John,
I hope my
story encourag

story

18+

Be Strong!

Never Quit.

Contact me @
Johnrmouser@gmail.com

MW01287335

18+

From Addiction to Addition

John Mouser

High Bridge Books
Houston

CONTENTS

Preface

This book came from a dream I had back in 2010. In my dream, I saw this book with a white cover with black letters that read, "18+." When I woke up, I thought, "Man, I wonder if that's on Amazon." So, I looked it up. Nothing was available, so I thought for several days about it. Then, I got the revelation the Lord was trying to show me. I counted on my fingers and found out that I had been addicted to mind-altering substances for 18 years. The "+" represented the freedom, joy, and blessing I would be able to walk in by becoming addicted to Jesus instead of substances that left me empty, time and time again.

Part 1

The Choice of Addiction

In 1991, I was a 9-year-old boy whose life was full of anger, unforgiveness, rejection, and a strong need for validation. My dad and I had a pretty good relationship. He used to tell me he loved me, which meant the world to me. Though, when I was 9 years old, he stopped.

My Uncle Larry always told me how much he loved me, gave me piggyback rides, and taught me things. He became my new role model. My uncle wasn't a good influence in my life, but he was an influence nonetheless. He began teaching me the wrong things. When I was four years old, I went to my first bar. My Uncle Larry took me everywhere he went, bad or good.

At the age of 9, I smoked my first cigarette, a Pall Mall to start my life off. At this time, I watched my first rated-R movie. What a little rebel I was. I had a little help from my uncle on those two.

My Aunt Sarah and Uncle Larry lived in Cedar Grove on West 74th and Wallace St., so I always stayed over at their house. Cedar Grove is a neighborhood in Shreveport, Louisiana that has been known for gangs, drugs, and violence. I was watching rated-R movies, smoking Pall Malls, and living by my own rules. I knew that if I wanted it, I could get it. I started to get into trouble more and more the older I got.

Being Taught Well

My mother and father raised me to go to church and know God. Proverbs 22:6 says, "Train a child in the way he should go, and when he is old, he will not depart from it." At a church function one night, I felt like I needed to give my heart to God. I kind of knew what it meant, so I confessed Jesus and was baptized to start my new journey off.

I really enjoyed hanging out at church. I would get in a lot of trouble though. Sometimes, I would think, "I'm just a kid. Let me just be a kid." One Wednesday night, my aunt and I got up on stage and sang my mom's favorite song to her. The song was called, "Thank You." She cried the entire time we sang. This was a very big step for me. I was so scared of being on stage.

While I was attending church, I made some close friends, one in particular that I would never forget. The kid's name was Aaron. We were always at each other's houses. One Sunday morning, the altar call went forth. I looked up, and Aaron was down in the front, weeping in front of the whole church. As I looked at my best friend, God said to my heart, "I'm calling you into the ministry just like I just called him."

From that day forward, I did everything I could to mute the voice of God, trying to disqualify myself from becoming a pastor. I mean, come on. I was only a 10-year-old brat. What could God do with my life? I quit attending church from that point forward. I began pursuing the life of a thug and rebel. Little did I know, it would lead me down a rough path. And so, my prodigal son story began.

Wanting Attention

Everywhere I went, I would act out and make a scene. One evening, while riding in my dad's new truck, my mom told me that I couldn't go hang with street friends anymore. In retaliation, I kicked the windshield, shattering it. Then, I got out of the truck and plowed the door with my knee about five times, leaving major damage.

For years, I verbally abused my parents and tried to dominate their household as a young boy. Some nights, I would verbally abuse my mom to the point of her crying herself to sleep. I had become a monster.

As a 14-year-old boy, my life was surrounded by violence, drugs, sexual activity, alcohol, anger, and rage. I wanted more every day. I wanted so bad to be accepted and cool, so I began to hang around gang members at school. The gang of choice was the Rollin 60 Crips. I felt like I was *somebody* when I was hanging out with them.

My mom couldn't control me. I was coming home at four or five o'clock in the morning at 15 years old on school nights, so she called my counselor from school to assist. Mr. Hite was a large man, full of authority, and we had a decent friendship because I stayed in trouble at school. He would come to the house and talk to me, trying to bring some discipline to keep me from going down the wrong road in life which I would later travel. Drugs, stealing, fighting, and partying would be my next turn in life. It would start out fun but end in disaster.

I was always stealing things. Once, I stole some caution lights from a construction site. The sheriff didn't find that too funny. As I was returning home on the bus one day back in middle school, I saw that my driveway was full of cops. The sheriff told me that if I didn't return the caution lights, he would arrest me on a felony charge as a thief, and jail would be my home.

Everywhere I went, I was getting in trouble. I stayed in detention so much that I thought I could graduate with that one credit. If you don't feel you are getting enough attention at home, you will always search elsewhere. When I was a student at Huntington High School, I was hanging out with people twice my age. Some went to school. Some didn't. Some days, I would attend school. Some days, I would skip. The more drugs I did, the worse I went down. I got to the point one year that I was never sober at school. Some friends of mine figured we would get drunk while at school. Buy a coke. Fill it up with alcohol. Then, we'd just party all day at school. When we got home, we'd do the same thing. During my 10th grade year, I didn't even show up.

Drop out

High school was not interesting enough for me, so I dropped out and moved to the hood where I had spent most of my days. I moved in with my Aunt Sarah. She was a second mom to me. However, she was not much of a good influence on me due to the lack of accountability. Plus, she lived in the hood where I could get any drug I wanted. I was a bad influence on many others, so they moved in with me. The heavy partying went on all day—everyday.

In just a matter of three months, it was estimated that we spent $20,000 on drugs and alcohol. Gone. Totally wasted away.

My whole sophomore year was spent doing whatever, whenever, and however I wanted. This gave me an invincibility mentality. My friends all dropped out with me and began the spiral of being rebels, following nobody's rules and living for what we wanted. We would rap, smoke, drink, shop, play with our guns, play dice, and play dominos. We always toted our pistols around, just in case someone had a problem. We wanted to live the life we saw on TV. The more bad stuff we did, the more exciting it became. We were always going further, trying new things to *one up* the last guy, showing him who was the baddest guy on the block.

One day, I was sitting outside with my friends, Monsta and 12, drinking on some Thunderbird. We got to talking about life, and 12 said, "JSlim, you need to cool out on all the drama, or you going to get smoked in this neighborhood." I didn't really think he knew who he was messing with, but my boy was telling me the truth, so I heard him out. We hung out everyday. He was a rapper, and he was a good one. We were listening to the radio one day, and they played his song. Oh buddy, we started dancing and singing like we were at a concert. I respected 12. He knew how to handle himself. He took care of his mom. He never disrespected her in front of me, and he wasn't trying to be somebody else. He knew who he was and was totally cool with that. He really looked after me like a little brother. It's a good thing because I had a smart mouth and a really bad temper.

One night, I drank way too much of this malt liquor, and this guy rolls by on his bike. Like always, I stared him down. I mean, he was rolling through my block, so I can stare. He popped off something, and I was headed for him. It was a miracle that 12 was outside because I was going to pull out my pistol and put a few bullets in the air.

I had a big problem with running my mouth and not thinking things through. I thought I was King Kong everywhere I went. My aunt would tell me, "Boy, you wasn't born on a silver platter." My family couldn't believe how I had turned out. After all, nobody taught me to be a rebel. I just chose that way myself.

I have two sisters that are older than me. Growing up, I already felt like the black sheep, being a boy. One sister is 12 years older, and the other is 8 years older. As brothers and sisters, we went through our fights and arguments. I terrorized them, and they terrorized me. We all survived and have all of our limbs. Life is good.

My oldest sister seemed to have a heart for me as little brat brother, so she would check up on me from time to time through all of my rebel days. One day, as I was living in the hood, doing what I knew best to do, big sis stopped by for a talk. This wasn't a nice talk. It was more of a "come to Jesus" meeting. She shared truth with me, letting me know that my future did not look so hot with the path I was choosing.

I used to wear Dickies, Airmax's, hat sideways, blue do-rag in the back pocket, and a pistol in the waist, locked and loaded. My boys, Jerk and 12, taught me that life in the hood is every man for himself. You walk around with your heat and always watch your back. Never trust anybody out here in the streets. You have to make a living out here by slinging drugs, running blocks, or robbing folks. I figured that couldn't be too hard. I had no education, no job, no self-control, and no discipline.

A life full of drugs, alcohol, and destruction is not the proper way to bring success to your life. For sure.

John Mouser

A small change for the good

When my oldest sister, Melanie, came by the hood to speak with me, she set me straight. I knew she was right by calling me *trash*. I mean, I had nothing to live for. No destiny. Just waking up, tossing the dice, and living on the edge.

She offered for me to move to her home and go back to school. I could get a great start in the right direction. Of course, this would be a major adjustment. Going from thug life to pretty boy life wouldn't be easy.

On the night before the first day back to high school, I was so nervous. I didn't want to get in a fight, get kicked out, waste my sister's time, be picked on, or anything else. I made up my mind that I would begin to make right choices, get my education, pay tickets back, complete probation, maintain a job, etc.

On the second day of Parkway High School, I met a girl, and she was cute. Being the charmer I was, I started to put my mack game down. You know, new boy in town, show me around. Come to find out, this girl had a man and never told me about it, nor did I ask. So, I'm sitting in gym class, and the whole football team walks up to me, and this one little guy says, "Hey, I heard you talking to my girl." Classic high school stuff. I told him I didn't hear her say she had a man. Now, the ideal thing to say in this moment is, "Yea man, I sure am sorry about that. It was a misunderstanding, so you can keep your teeth in your mouth." Well, the guy just walked off, but I knew that wasn't going to be the end of that.

A few weeks went by, and she didn't look my way much, nor did I speak to her. Come to find out, the guy that was going to try to give me a beating that day is related to my sister's friend. So, we let it all go out the window and began hanging out. This guy here was a party animal, so I got hooked right back in the same cycle I just came out of. The only difference was that I was in a different area code.

I slowly began to notice that if I wanted to be somebody different, I had to make the adjustments myself. Everyone that I knew did all the same things though: party, drink, smoke, and date all the beautiful girls you can. My neighbor, Nick, was one of the most popular guys at my school, so all I had to do was hang out with him, and girls would flock to me. Getting girls was a major reason why I did most the things I did. The ultimate cure for rejection is acceptance.

While I was in school, I took a trade class where they taught us different skills. I chose to learn auto body. It worked out very well for me. I painted my own car while in the class. This led me to a job working on Lexus cars, doing painting, body work, and restoration for around 10 years.

Back to full throttle addiction

After I graduated, I moved back to the hood while I was working. It was only me and my auntie living there, so it was cool. I was pretty free to do anything I wanted because I was working. I was making incredible money working on Lexus cars. I had no rent to pay—just tickets, fines, and probation. I blew every check on partying, as usual. I had the usual keg parties every weekend. You know, just getting back to the regular.

Then, it began to get out-of-hand with the drugs being added in again. I was drinking and driving very frequently. I figured that because I had cleaned up, I could do the crime and not have to do the time. I would just move a few bucks around to sling drugs—no major shipments or noticeable amounts. For safety reasons, I was only in it for the party hype.

My aunt began to grow impatient with my lifestyle, so we started to butt heads. She would try to limit me, so I hit the road.

Let me teach you something real quickly. Aunt

Sarah was indeed an enabler in my life. My mom played a major part as well. So, honestly I had two enablers. When I couldn't manipulate one, I would manipulate the other. Enablers tend to chase after the addict, giving he or she whatever they need so that they will be safe or provided for. This just fuels the addict into deeper addiction. The more people cater to the addict's destructive lifestyle, the longer the addict is able to live in addiction, free from responsibility or consequences. When the addict has no one to use, steal from, or manipulate, he or she is driven towards needing an intervention. I knew that my mom or my aunt would always bail me out. They had been bailing me out since I was a toddler.

I was dating a girl that had a place, so I moved in over there. From that point, I lived the married life minus the rings. We were together for about a year. For me, that was a super long time. Then, unfortunately for her, I turned 21. I had always gone to the clubs, but now it was much easier. One night, my brother-in-law took me out, and man, we drank everything but the rain water on the ground and the water in the toilets. When I woke up the next day, I was super glad I didn't have anyone beside me. My girlfriend called and called and called, so I picked up then had her come pick me up. Thankfully, I had not cheated on her that night. Good boy. Always try to do the basics. Not really.

My buddies began to convince me to go to the strip club with them. Well, you see, I didn't need convincing. I was down before they asked me. One weekend, we planned on going, but we all had girlfriends that hung out together, so our story had to match up. I told my girlfriend we were going to the bar, so off we went. I pretty much spent every dime I had in my pocket at the strip club. Good thing I didn't have our rent money because I would have spent that, too.

A week later, my girlfriend asked me if I enjoyed myself that night when I spent our $600 spending money for the month. I laughed and said, "Yea, we had a great time at that bar."

"Well," she said, "Are you sure it was just a bar?"

"Well, duh," I said. "Oh yea, it was definitely a bar."

She said, "That's not what your boy, Curtis, said."

I knew I was busted now. I said, "Look, we went to the strip club and stayed there all night 'til I came home."

Yes, you're right. She was crazy raging mad. I would have been, too. I made a pretty good liar, and I would have taken that to the grave. My friend,

Curtis, decided he didn't want to do that. So, we all got in trouble. From that point on, trust was majorly damaged.

I manipulated her to stay with me until I found another girl to be with. I did find another one and immediately moved in with her, mainly because my girlfriend found out she had stayed the night at our house while she was out of town for her work. Well, I wasn't faithful to any other girl, so why should I start now? The bad thing is that I really did care about my girlfriend, but I was not in the shape to try maintaining anything that would last forever. My new girlfriend would party with me. She did whatever I said, so she was definitely cool.

Drug dealing

I began to go over to a really close friend's house, P-Dog, more than I usually would. We had been friends since I was a child. He was my absolute best friend. We would die for one another, fight for one another, and spend big money on one another. There are not many friends you find like that. We were more like brothers.

He began to push some heavy drug weight from state to state. As I would visit, he began to be very wealthy—like, very wealthy. We rented this car one weekend. It was a brand new Nissan Maxima. This car was beautiful. We hopped in and blasted to a low rider show in Texas. The car was full of drugs and cash, so we knew it was on. We bought all kinds of hydraulics, wheels, and shirts—whatever we wanted. We knew we were limited because we drove a car here, so we couldn't get too crazy.

When we got home, I knew I wanted to be a part of whatever he was doing, including fixing up an old school car with rims, a paint job, and hydraulics. So, we began to live the big life back in our hometown. Business as usual.

Part 2

The Consequences of Addiction

I began to hit up the clubs pretty heavily, staying out all hours of the day and night again. I was making strong connections with the underground world but still staying underneath the radar. I hung out with the in-crowd all the time: big ballers, shot callers, deep pocket boys, buy the whole club out kind of folks, etc.

My best friend and I began to start going a little deeper then we had ever gone before in our pursuit of quick success. Trying to take over new territory in the drug world was a big risk we were willing to take. We really never meant to become criminals, but when you are going all in, there will always be risks. Shipments were coming in as planned. As we built our reputation around the city, business was good. The biggest challenge was to get the drugs in and get rid of them as quickly as possible. The more parties we found, the faster we got rid of our product. All of us had a big speaker box, so guess where the drugs went during transport. There you go.

I had quit working for the Lexus shop to pursue more money because $900 a week was chump change. I went to work with a friend, installing alarm systems for hotels and casinos. We went out to just enjoy ourselves and our money. On one night before we left the house, we drank a whole fifth of Hennessy. On the way there, we smoked a good bit of marijuana. We finally made it to the club, and we were way under the influence. We asked the bartender for Jose Cuervo tequila. Well, he already made a drink with a cheaper tequila. So, he said, "Pay for this drink. Then, I'll make you another." I can't believe he thought this was going to happen.

So, we said, "No, you make my drink how I want it."

Well, the bartender got mad and tried to come over the bar. Bad news for him. I had an empty glass in my right hand. As he came over, I planted my glass between his eyeballs, and my friend gave me a few head bounces off the floor with his elbow. Seconds later, we were being escorted out by two massive security officers. My friend came out missing a shoe, and I came out talking smack. As we were walking to the car, I saw a bunch of guys that were staring, so I told all 9 of them, "You got a problem? Let's go!"

My friend said, "Don't worry about him. He had way too much to drink."

We made it back home with the help of his girlfriend. We continued to sell drugs as usual to provide for our Hollywood lifestyles.

Invitation to church

On a service call, I went to this church place for college students Baptist Collegiate Ministries. When I got there, I immediately put up a wall, mainly because I felt that church was full of a bunch of hypocrites pretending to be good when they do the same stuff I do. So, I talked with the guy who ran the place, Billy, while I worked on their alarm.

Before I left, he said, "Hey bud, what you doing tonight?"

I said, "Not too much."

So, he invited me to come and play pool with them at 7:00pm. When I got in the van, I knew what I was going to be doing at 7:00pm and that was receiving a shipment of drugs.

Busted

That July evening went more than a little unplanned. We arrived at the spot where we would be setup by a confidential informant from the ATF. I was handcuffed at 7:00pm sharp when I should have been at Baptist Collegiate Ministries. We were raided with 44 pounds of marijuana and a firearm on-hand. The reality never hit until days later, but we were exposed with a pretty major shipment. It's not so good for business as your sales career comes to a crashing halt, and you're handed over to the judicial system for polluting their city. As I reached for the phone at the Caddo Parish Correctional Center, the seriousness of my actions hit me.

Doing time

The phone call I was about to make to my mom would totally crush her. All I've been taught. All they worked for. All they fought for. It would be destroyed in one call. So, I dialed the number, hitting the last button in shame.

"Mom, I'm in jail," I said.

"Oh no, honey, what happened?"

"I've been selling drugs, and I won't be getting out of here for quite some time," I said.

She only wept in silence. I could hear her fear in her crying. "I'm sorry" is all I could think to say, which meant nothing most the time.

The court wouldn't do much for us. We watched our stories play over and over again on the local news, day after day.

When I entered my cell, I met Abraham. He was

going to be my new roommate. Abraham knew I was in big trouble when I told him about my charge. On the first night, I wept all night because I felt the consequences of my actions. I felt like Jonah when he was swallowed up by the whale, except I wasn't in a whale but in a cold jail. God told Jonah to go to Nineveh. At first, he wasn't willing to go. Then, after some time in a whale, he decided he would obey after all.

I thought that we would never see the light of day again. Abraham began to tell me I needed to cry out to God and seek His Word for direction. We began to have Bible studies and talk about life, good experiences and bad experiences. It seemed like time went by faster just having fun with each other.

My cell neighbor's nickname was "6." He was about to do 14 years, so he was pretty laid back. No reason to get in a hurry. It was already home sweet home from the start for 6. We got to know each other pretty well. I found out that he knew some of the same people I kicked it with.

I got moved from cell to cell because of the amount of inmates in there. I met this one guy named Jonathon. He was so cool. We had a blast. He was about my age, so we clicked immediately. He was in on an armed robbery charge, looking at about 10 years. He had a cousin named, Mayfield. He did all the hair cutting up there. Jonathon and I got some rubber bands from the commissary and began putting our hair in rows. This was hilarious for me, but if my boy does it, I have to do it.

The day of court arrived, and they just pushed the date off until the following month. Our bond was set at $250,000, so there was no one who could get us out. As we were adjusting to our new home, my friends and I found it tough to be calm about our case. Our minds wondered if we would ever get out. Worry was my friend, along with fear. We had no hope. No chance. The situation wasn't very good for us.

The jail offered an evening of recreation time where you could watch TV, play board games, make phone calls, etc. Some got the chance to experience this. Others that are in solitary confinement just watch from a 13x2" Plexiglas window.

We would often have visitors on our scheduled day, which was based on our last name. Mom would come and send friends to visit me. It was awfully hard to watch her from the other side of the glass. Disappointment, shame, and guilt all filled me up when I would see people from the outside come visit. It would almost have been better just to be around other people in the jail, who shared the same feelings I had.

In jail, there is a code and system. If you mind your own business, everything can go well for you. On the other hand, if you act a fool, you'll have a rather tough stay. I chose to be pretty calm and let my time serve me well. At first, it didn't happen like that. I was rowdy, feeling like I had to make a scene to show everyone I was hardcore and wasn't going to take any junk off anyone.

Divine Intervention

The Lord allowed me to get hooked up with some great guys in jail. They taught me about the Bible, what they knew from a real life perspective. I learned that we are not condemned by God, but we are accepted. He paid the price so we can have new life. The fresh start, born again experience was for me as I was full of sin, shame, regret, greed, adultery, and addiction. I could come to Him, and He would wash me clean and give me a brand new life. My mess qualified me to receive His love, acceptance, forgiveness, freedom, peace, rest, strength, and everything else He offers. Jesus came for the sick, not for those who think they're "good enough."

I had never ever heard this before. At least, I never listened. They had Wednesday church service and Sunday services in the cage house. I would call jail the *cage house* from time to time. I felt like a bird in a cage at times. I wanted to fly away. I began to sing in the choir on Wednesday nights in jail. In the *Book of Acts*, Paul and Silas were singing to the Lord, chained up. Yet, they could still touch Jesus and feel His presence as they entered into worship in jail. Then, the cell doors opened and the jailer even got saved. Then, they were released. God doesn't leave anyone out. That is majorly encouraging. I loved reading the Psalms and Proverbs from my Bible. I quoted Psalm 31 everyday with passion.

Every day, I was trying to make the best of my time being locked up and trying to help my cell mate stay encouraged about his situations going on outside the jail walls. We began to have these prayer calls on the basketball court. There would be about 60 of us locked shoulder to shoulder in a huddle, praying about our families, murder charges, felony convictions, grace on our trials, and whatever else we had on our hearts. It was fresh. It brought me peace and helped me to deal with the weight of possibly having to make jail my home for a long time.

Philippians 1:6 says, "Being confident of this very thing, that he who has begun a good work in you will complete it until the day of Jesus Christ." No matter what I did, he would still complete the work that got started in that jailhouse.

Jail Sentencing

Whether the sentence would be 40 years, 15 years, or 10 years, I was trying to set a good pace for myself. Court date after court date, we would get pushed off to the next month. We were being charged with possession of schedule 1 with the quantity of 44 pounds of marijuana (5-10 years sentence) and illegal carrying of weapons (15-30 years sentence).

The Feds came to change our wristbands from red to green, which would take our case from state to federal. It happened! Green means you have to appear before the federal court instead of state. In our case, that was at least a 10-year sentence. The names were called for court, but I didn't hear my name. It was the day I waited for. My boys got called, but I had been forgotten.

My sister's husband had left her, my mom had been sick, and my aunt had been real sick. It was chaos. As I looked out my cell window, I began to weep with anger. "God! This is supposed to be my day of freedom!" Out of rage, I tore up my cell, flipped the boxes and punched the concrete walls over and over again! Weeping, I felt hopeless. I'll never get back to my life! I'm trapped in this cycle like a sheep to the slaughterhouse.

I laid on my bunk for about 10 minutes, weeping. Then, *pop!* My door opened! "Mouser! Come on! They are waiting on you!" We flew in that Ford van, all chained together, 10 deep. With shackles on my ankles and my hands cuffed to my belt strap, I walked into the court room, expecting my freedom to be granted. After all, I had been praying and trying to do the right thing, so why shouldn't I be released?

The judge said, "Why should I let you out of jail today?"

I said, "Judge, I met Jesus, and I am wanting to make a new picture of my life." Immediately, he said, "Everyone meets Jesus in jail. I hear that story every day. Sit down." The attorney came and sat beside me after a long day of court. They had us in a glass room separated from the people so they could see us, and we could see them. My attorney said, "John, you will go back to work tomorrow." Inside, I felt a flood of emotions.

When I got back to my pod, the section of the jail I had been living in, I was pumped because they released me on a ROR bond. This meant they just had to do some paperwork, and then I would be released. There was no money to pay. So, I gave all my snacks away to the other guys because I was about to be history. It's like waiting on your number and then moving on to the next destination.

Have you ever been to jail or a detention center?

Have your actions ever caused your family damage?

Part 3

The Chains of Addiction

Boom! My door popped, and I was in the Sally port. I remember my Christian friends from jail saying, "Don't forget what you learned and Who got you out." I was thinking, "There's no way I'll ever forget that God granted my freedom. I'm going to be walking a different walk now."

As soon as I got out, I saw my Aunt Sarah. I knew it was on then. I smelled the outside air. Wow! It was fresh and great. Then, I hopped in truck, and we were off. It seemed like cars got bigger, and they were super loud to me now. Because we didn't hear many loud noises in jail, our ears were sensitive. Aunt Sarah threw me a pack of cigarettes, and I busted them open. As I smoked the first one, I felt lightheaded immediately. Wow! Like the first time. We pulled into Ryan's Steakhouse and headed to have my first real meal outside the concrete walls. Being a goofball, I ordered a large steak, mashed potatoes, and roll. Well, I ate the potatoes and didn't even touch the steak. My stomach was shrunk.

We headed back to the hood to get all setup for life once again. I called the boss and let him know I'm back on the map. I gathered all my belongings and then settled down for the evening. It took a few days off to get things lined up to return back to putting alarms back in around the city. I had a court date set for the next month, so I was back to the normal life. All of my friends began to come by and want to talk about all that been taking place. So, I sat on the back porch chilling with them, having a few cold ones as the sun went down.

Back to the basics

My cousin was in town from the Navy, so we had to get in some trouble. Whether it was wrecking a car, sinking a car, getting pulled over, going mud riding, driving on the sand bar, or getting in a fight, it was going to be a fun night. We went out and met up with a large group of people to go to the clubs in the city. As the night went on, I began to loosen up and have a few drinks. Well, that got to be a habit once again.

When you get out of jail, your tolerance for alcohol is super low. So, I was plowed within 15 minutes of drinking some tequila, puked on the family dog, fell into the wall, and knocked a body size hole in it. They had to bring me home with a trash bag taped to my face to keep me from throwing up everywhere. I woke up the next morning, wondering if this was the life I was going to live forever.

I had been resting all day when a friend of mine brought a book over to me titled, *The Purpose Driven Life*. I wasn't much into church stuff because I felt they wouldn't accept me, always trying to change me, judge me, and look at me like they had seen a ghost. I read the book while I was really stoned one night to see what it was all about. It is a great book, for real. It helped me see that we have to make something of our lives on earth. I definitely didn't know where to start.

I continued on my own, street partying, hoping that I would run into my purpose. I would often think that I would find a great girl in the midst of my bar scene or through friends, but that never worked out. It would last for a few months, but I never trusted them, or I would try to control them. I wanted a thriving, healthy relationship. Life seemed so redundant, partying Friday and Saturday, then a little church on Sunday. I grew tired of the mundane life. I knew in my heart that there was more to life than what I was experiencing. I began to search the Bible. I grabbed some good knowledge but not much.

War in the City

One evening, my cousin and I were partying with some girls, and we were both pretty intoxicated. Our judgment was off. We found ourselves in a bad situation. These guys at the party didn't like other guys from another part of town. That happened to be where we were from. So, we felt cornered. It was three of us against 30 of them. We began to defend what little ground we had, which didn't last long at all.

There we were in the hospital, trying to get all stitched up. This brewed some serious anger in us. We called all our friends from school and some of the baddest dudes we knew to meet up and find the guys that beat us up. We rode all night looking for any of them, probably 50-60 deep. It looked like a funeral procession without the police escort. We were unsuccessful until we saw a guy at the gas station that looked like one of the guys, so we jumped in the car and chased him down. They got away, and we were unable to send the message out that we weren't going to be beaten and not give a beating back.

When I got home, I was confronted with all kinds of stuff about the guy being scared we were going to kill him and his friends. It would have been the arrogant thing to retaliate as most men do. I chose for the first time in my life to let it go and be a real man.

Bailed Out

One night, all of my buddies and I got together to go to a bar to celebrate—as if we really needed a reason to celebrate. This bar served these awesome margaritas, and if you know me, I loved margaritas. I had about five of them, which is entirely too much.

Somehow, I caught up with my friends when I was done with my margarita binge. We all decided that it was club time, so all eight of us hopped up into this jacked-up Ford Super Duty. There was just one problem. None of us could determine who was sober enough to drive. I volunteered to drive this big ole' boss truck. So, I put the seatbelt on, and we smashed out like we robbed the place. I didn't get two miles down the road before I remembered I was on probation. Before I could pull over, I heard the *whoop whoop* from the police car that was behind me. I'm thinking, "Just don't slur, don't fall, and don't black out." Go. I got out kind of rough, and my foot got caught. I walked around the back of the truck, and the cop said, "You having trouble keeping that thing on the road son?"

I said, "Well, it is a monster truck, sir."

Sometimes you should think before you speak was my thought now.

He said, "You had anything to drink?"

I said, "Absolutely. Five margaritas."

He laughed and said, "Can I give you a field sobriety test?"

I assured him, "There is no need for that. I am toast."

He said, "Have a seat on the curb."

After that, he placed me in handcuffs and read my rights to me. I sat there thinking, "John, how do you consistently screw up?" I felt like God started speaking to me, but why would He bother me in a moment like this? I'm drunk. I'm driving drunk. I haven't been going to church. I only pray when I need something, and then I throw God back into closet when He makes all things better. I kept hearing this phrase: "Ask him to let one of your friends drive you home." So, I was going to try it because I was about to go to jail for DWI and then get charged with violating my probation. Double trouble.

He stepped out of the car and said, "Is this your current address?"

I said, "No, I am living with a friend." I proceeded, "Sir, can one of my friends just drive us home? I stay like two streets over." He laughed and returned to his car as I figured. Well it was worth a shot.

He got back out and said, "Boy, I've been having a really good night, so if you can find one sober guy in that truck, I'll let him drive you home." I knew one guy that was the one for the job. His name was Trey. He wasn't drunk, but he definitely wasn't sober. Trey had taken some X-tabs earlier, so I was hoping he wouldn't see any purple elephants crossing the road during his sobriety test. Can you believe he let that boy drive us home? Well, with the help of me driving from the passenger seat, we made it safely.

I knew that God was on to me and had totally bailed me out again, showing His love and mercy once again. Even while I was still a screw-up, Jesus bailed me out. The Bible puts it like this: "But God demonstrates his own love toward us, in that while we were still sinners, Christ died for us" (Rom. 5:8). The guys could not believe that this happened.

The Prodigal Son Returns

From that day, I went to church to see what business God wanted with me. I was tired of this lifestyle. It always left me empty. Temporary fun. Temporary pleasure. Everybody is drinking, but still they are not happy, nor are they anywhere close to fulfilling any meaningful purpose in life. So, I began to make some adjustments to get the results I desired.

I called an old friend that I knew was in church, and she invited me to her Bible study at a local coffee shop. When I went, I met some guys who were in a faith-based rehab program, and they were excited to be off drugs. Like, overly excited. These were the types of guys I prayed that God would bring into my life, so I could stay doing the right things. Well, I went bowling with them, and I actually had fun with a group of Christian guys. Definitely strange. These boys didn't smoke, cuss, or disrespect others. They just honored each other and spoke love to each other. I was weirded-out, big time. They would always talk about the presence of God. When they would ride to places, they would have worship music playing.

They were relentless about me coming to their church. I was already attending a church, but I wasn't connected, so I was lost in the loop. I said, "Yea, I'll go, man." But I really didn't want to. The next Sunday, we walked in as a group, like 5 deep. As soon as I walked in, I felt this love surround me. It was something I had never felt before.

The Bible has a story in Luke, Chapter 15, about the prodigal son that returned to his father's house.

It says, "So he returned home to his father. And while he was still a long way off, his father saw him coming. Filled with love and compassion, he ran to his son, embraced him, and kissed him." I began to weep as I walked to find a seat. I was really trying to hold back and be hard. I couldn't do it, so right there in my pew, I lifted my hands for the first time and told God, "Here I am! Take me and use me! I give up!" So, in July 2007, I was born again.

From that moment forward, I knew God had a hold of me stronger than any human ever had. I had no idea how to do church or know Jesus. The Bible tells us that "God chose things the world considers foolish in order to shame those who think they are wise" (1 Cor. 2:27). I definitely felt like one of those "foolish things." I began to hang out with this crowd called Christians. Man, I tell you. They were a different bunch. I expected them to be cussing and smoking cigarettes. You know, doing the church obligation on Sundays and Wednesdays. No, these were crazy Christians. They were hanging out Monday through Friday and then on weekends. That was a little much for me.

I still had some things I wasn't willing to let go of: some girls that were potential wives and a few old friends that were truly friends, but they weren't headed in the same direction. God began to connect me to some more people. I allowed Him to work on the rough places of my life that I had lived with for so long.

Have you ever been a prodigal son/daughter?

Have you ever surrendered to God totally?

Have you started adjusting your lifestyle? How could you start today?

Addiction

Addicts are people that lose things because of their habits, and they don't change. They also are people who genuinely want to stop, but they don't or can't. Some addictions are passed on from the parent to the child. The child observes the addiction of their parent, so they default to become one as well.

It's a common story in rehabs and treatment centers. Drug overdose was the leading cause of injury death in 2010. Among people 25 to 64 years old, drug overdose caused more deaths than motor vehicle traffic crashes. In 2011, about 1.4 million emergency department visits involved the non-medical use of pharmaceuticals. Among those ED visits, 501,207 visits were related to anti-anxiety and insomnia medications, and 420,040 visits were related to opioid analgesics. Every day in the United States, 105 people die as a result of drug overdose, and another 6,748 are treated in emergency departments for the misuse or abuse of drugs.

Addiction is the most misunderstood disease in the world. The addict sees and feels the effect of the addiction disease. Addiction has killed more people than cancer. We treat cancer as a life-threatening disease when spotted. Likewise, addiction is also a serious disease that if not dealt with quickly and properly, it will get worse and can result in death.

In 2011, an estimated 21.6 million Americans needed treatment for a problem related to drugs or alcohol, but only 2.3 million received treatment at a specialty facility. These numbers do not include any other addicts like pornography addicts, food addicts, sex addicts, internet or social media addicts, video game addicts, or work addicts. Addiction is indeed a disease that is killing millions of Americas daily. From the outside, addicts may not look sick, but on the inside, the addiction is rotting their body and stealing life the longer they remain addicted. Addicts may be doctors, teachers, principals, professional athletes, lawyers, council men, or coaches. Addicts will scheme, rob, and kill for drugs.

Employers with successful drug-free workplace programs report improvements in morale and productivity, and decreases in absenteeism, accidents, downtime, turnover, and theft. Addicts become isolated due to their addiction. They feel guilty and shameful because of their actions resulting from their addiction. Addiction takes a people farther than they want to go and keeps them there longer than they want to stay.

There are different stages of addiction just like there are for cancer or any other life-threatening disease. The mind is affected by the disease as much as the body is. Many addictions start out as a desire that got out of balance. Then, the desire begins to control the individual, dictating what they do on a daily basis. Intravenous drug users often shoot dope 10-12 times in one day to maintain their addiction.

I began to wonder how the Bible could help me with my addiction. Addiction in its simplest form boils down to death: "But each one is tempted when he is drawn away by his own desires and enticed. Then, when desire has conceived, it gives birth to sin; and sin, when it is full-grown, brings forth death" (Jam. 1:14-15). Having sin and death in my life, I needed to find a way to conquer them. Paul writes,

"Oh what a miserable person I am! Who will free me from this life that is dominated by sin and death? Thank God! The answer is in Jesus Christ our Lord. So you see how it is: In my mind I really want to obey God's law, but because of my sinful nature I am a slave to sin." (Rom. 7:24-25)

I am going to have to fight these desires and refuse to give in to my sinful nature. That totally made sense to me. I can be free by saying "no" to my desires to use drugs and alcohol. I never could make it that far to say "no." The desire would present itself to me, so I would give in to make it go away. Now, I just have to fight the desire and say "no."

Then, I discovered this promise from God's Word: "And because you belong to him, the power of the life-giving spirit has freed you from the power of sin that leads to death" (Rom. 8:2). Major game-changer! When the desire comes, I need to respond with the Spirit of God inside me, declaring that I have been freed from the power of addiction and its desires. Daily, I had to remind my sinful nature that I had been freed from drugs, alcohol, nicotine, pornography, and all other selfish desires. This was a process and required much accountability over a period of time until I could stand on my own two feet.

Today, I still have to say "no" when my sinful nature tries to remind me of my past. I'm too busy headed to my glorious future that Jesus has for me to turn around to repeat my season of the build-up, tear-down cycle.

"Not that I have already attained, or am already perfected; but I press on, that I may lay hold of that for which Christ Jesus has also laid hold of me. Brethren, I do not count myself to have apprehended; but one thing I do, forgetting those things which are behind and reaching forward to those things which are ahead, I press toward the goal for the prize of the upward call of God in Christ Jesus." (Phil. 3:13-14)

Damage of Addiction

Most crimes are somehow drug-related. As I write this, I just saw in the news that a 16-year-old boy was robbing this grandma for the second time. As she was grabbing for the money he requested, she grabbed her gun and shot him several times in the chest, fatally wounding him. He ran out in the yard where he later died, with 55 cents in a bag next to him. The question is, was he robbing her to get money, to buy drugs, or maybe alcohol? We will never know because it cost him his life. The selfish desires of our flesh wanting to use drugs or alcohol leaves a huge wake of destruction as the addict chases fix after fix, always needing more as they drain family bank accounts, trust funds, and retirement accounts.

I was able to interview my mom one day to see how much my addiction really affected her. She began to tell me all the stories from my childhood as I progressed into an adult. She said, "I was under a lot of stress raising you." During my addiction, my mom had to endure shame, guilt, stress, verbal abuse, disrespect, health problems, anger, financial problems, loss of friends, feelings of betrayal, loneliness, and depression. She said, "John, you chose your friends over your family every time. We always tried to help you and love you but you pushed us aside." Mom was criticized by her own family when I went to jail. As the local news broadcast week after week the story of her son being involved in a drug raid, she wept alone. She made a statement one time when I was locked up that stuck with me forever: "John, you will never know what it's like to look at your baby boy and not be able to do anything to help him. It kills me to not know if I will ever be able to hug you again or smell you again. Can't you see how you are hurting me?" When I returned to my cell, I wept for hours for what I was doing to my family.

My father experienced grief and feelings of failure as a father even though he had done all he knew to do as a father. He said, "No matter what happens, we will just have to stand by him the best we can as a family." It really rocked my dad's world because he thought I was following in some of his footsteps. He wasn't sure what to do, watching me go through my messy addiction. He hoped that I would learn my lesson.

My Aunt Jenny had a rough time watching me decline in my addiction. She wanted to intervene several times but couldn't get through to me due to my stubborn, rebellious, and disrespectful attitude to those around me.

Recovery

Coming from the life of addiction, the former addict can have a great bit to offer current addicts. Oftentimes, I got opportunities to go and share my testimony at Eagle Creek Recovery Center. I have always been involved in helping them with their Tuesday night meetings. Whether it be vacuum cleaning, setting up chairs, plugging up a keyboard, making coffee, greeting new people, praying for people during prayer time, or taking roll at the door, I always found a place to serve and give back. I learned so much from the leaders out there. I was able to get free of all my addictions and bondages through their help in 2010.

At Eagle Creek, Ben teaches the 12 steps from a Biblical perspective. He encourages accountability and transparency during the whole process. If not for this step, I would never be where I am today. The question is not if you struggle; it's when you struggle. Being transparent about my temptations, wrong desires, and struggles helped me to feel normal, so I didn't hide or try to isolate (Jam. 5:16). Ben has the guys write a list of people that they have harmed, people that harmed them, people they need to forgive, and people they stole from. At that point, the guys write letters to those they harmed. If possible and appropriate, they will apologize face-to-face. This teaches the students to take total responsibility for their actions. This also helps them learn to clean up their own mess rather than depending on others to continue cleaning up their messes.

Ben had to pay people back that he stole money from in his addictive state. He said he wrote a letter to a girl that he robbed, telling her that he was sorry and that he wanted to make all the wrongs right. Her letter back to him was, "I would like you to begin to pay me my money back as you can." So, he did just that until they agreed the debt was indeed paid.

Consequences are what help the addict see the damage they caused around them due to their selfish choices. They also teach the addict while in recovery to be humble, relational, professional, responsible, and fruitful. The classes are designed to teach them how to do the work of recovery. Sitting in class is not recovery, but the active response to the material and engagement of the patient determines what they get from the program. A guy that totally surrenders to God's plan for his life during the recovery process listens to the wisdom offered from the leadership and completes all tasks requested from the program. He also enters a transitional living program. This way, he can get back on his feet, restored to society with accountability to handle the brand new pressures of a recovered addict. Ben says the guy that makes it this far normally gains more ground than he lost to begin with.

The teachings are simple, and the program is faith-based, founded on a relationship with Jesus Christ to remain in freedom from addiction. Taking the word of God and showing the addict how it can be applied to his life to start the process of healing and restoration is an everyday lesson in this program. The same materials are given week after week. The addict needs a rigorous schedule so that there is very little idle time to focus on anything that could derail the road to recovery.

They need to be taught how to think differently. Life has to be relearned. They must learn how to live for Christ, not for themselves. Selfishness is the path to destruction. Based on my own experience, I have seen the recovery process work like this:

1. Repentance from sin (Acts 3:19)
2. Receiving of new life in Christ (2 Cor. 5:17)
3. Addiction deliverance (Psa. 68:20)
4. Removal of death in my lifestyle (Matt. 3:8)
5. Freedom from all bondage and strongholds (Gal. 5:13)
6. Walking in the life of addition to my God, myself, and my family (Psa. 107:2)

When I was addicted, I didn't have a mission other than to get so medicated that I could block out reality. When I met Jesus, He empowered me with a mission in spite of my mess:

"Go therefore and make disciples of all the nations, baptizing them in the name of the Father and of the Son and of the Holy Spirit, teaching them to observe all things that I have commanded you; and lo, I am with you always, even to the end of the age." (Matt. 28:19-20)

He made me a part of something that didn't have to do with just me. I am called to go to the world and help people that are just like me, who found themselves in bad situations, losing their lives they worked so hard to keep and knowing they were meant to do much more than be addicted to drugs. The person that really gets down the road in a life of recovery is one who gets totally healed and restored and then makes it about helping other people getting healed and restored.

Addition

After getting set free from a life of destruction, addiction, and darkness through the power of the blood of Jesus Christ, I began to see myself becoming a new person. I was indeed being transformed from the inside out.

I thought different.

I felt different.

I talked different.

I looked different.

I walked different.

No longer did I have to fear returning to my old life of misery. I could live in freedom forever with a mind full of peace and a life full of treasure. I could watch every dream I ever had come to pass before my very eyes.

My family relationships began to be restored, starting with Mom. She was so glad to see me go to a church where they liked me, and I liked them. A church that didn't judge me for where I had been and all the mistakes I made.

My Aunt Jenny also got to see the transformation process. When she was in the hospital going through the trial of her life, she lost her eye to a flesh-eating disease called strep. I was driving down the street by the hospital where she was when the Lord told me put aside my offense, go in there, and pray for her. I said, "Heck no!" Then, I turned around after 10 minutes of driving, parked, and went to go find her in there. I walked into her room, and she was in bad shape to say the least. They couldn't control the disease that was eating her flesh around her eye. They hoped it wouldn't get to her brain.

I said, "Aunt Jenny, it's John here. I know we have had some tough encounters, but I only came here to pray for you. The Lord told me to stop in even when I didn't want to." From that day on, we were closer than we had ever been. She ended up getting healed although she lost her vision in one eye. We talk often at family gatherings.

Another story of addition is my father. Although it was tough to watch his son make a total mess of his life, he was glad to see me learn so much. He was excited to see me to do something with my life even when he didn't express it with words. I will never forget him saying when I was a little boy, "John, you will never grow up to be anything." Now, he couldn't be happier for me. He said, "John, I'm proud of you. I'm glad you're doing something for God and not for money." This statement shocked me. Most people tell us to do things that can help us get a lot of money. Dad knows the secret: if you do it for God, you will get much more than mere dollars.

Part 4

The Battle Against Addiction

The first person that began to show me what a true follower of Christ looks like was my boy, Miguel. Man, he let me know up front that living for Jesus was going to be hard and that it would cost me popularity, attention, and comfortability. I was like, "Hold the phone, man. I don't know if I want to pursue this if it's going to be a dead end road full of struggles." I stood by the fence of life, wondering whether to go all in for Christ or all in for the evil I had lived with for so long.

I still showed up at church and the life group Miguel connected me to. I began to wear down. My walls began to collapse. Walls of security I built to keep others from hurting me. Walls I built to be strong and tough at all times. Walls of saying everything is *okay* began to crumble.

As I was at church one day, the music was playing as usual, but something was taking place on the inside of me that I had never felt before. All my church buddies were sold out all the way for Jesus. Their hands were raised, singing to the top of their lungs because Jesus had set them free from so much. That wasn't my story yet, but I felt like it was about to be. So, I lifted my hands and began to sing. It was like a dam broke loose in me! Bam! There I was, crying like a baby. Singing and crying, I was a mess. I felt so much better, though. So much peace. So much rest and joy. I told Jesus, "Come set me free from my addictions. Give me strength to want to live for You. I just want live for me. Help me understand what's going on because I'm brand new at this." Yet, it was so simple, not complicated.

Getting Connected

Jesus answered my prayer. About a month later, I got invited to a discipleship group to learn more about Jesus, how to be follower of Christ, and how to obey God. I knew it was Him opening the door. So, I went on a Thursday night. It was held at Matt and Britnye's grandparents' house. It was called a home *life group*. They allow you to get to know so many people in the church. Especially when on any given Sunday there are 1,500 to 2,000 people at church, it's impossible to connect with everybody at church in a deep way. We each need a life group.

The first night was amazing. We listened to some worship music, and then Matt began to speak on issues that he went through in his walk with God. Then, Britnye began to speak on her encounters throughout her walk with God. Well, I had only been born again for about six months, so I'm soaking all this up. Very practical stuff they shared. I learned about the power of forgiveness, which began the healing and restoration of relationships with my Dad, Mom, and Grandfather. I was indeed becoming new. Like Jesus said, "Behold, I am making all things new!"

Matt came to me afterward and asked me where I was serving in church, and I was like, "Um, nowhere. I serve the pew pretty well!" He invited me to be a part of the CREW. During the church services, CREW ran the lights, moved instruments, changed microphone batteries, ran computers, carried the podium, and did other things like that. I said, "Yes, I would love to do that."

Junk Yard Ministry

One night, the Lord spoke to my heart and said, "John, you are going to own a body shop one day." I'm like, "Awesome! When do I get started?" At this time, I was working for a salvage yard, driving a front-end loader, crushing cars. So, I would work outside all day and then have my commitments in the evenings. I specifically did that, so I wouldn't have much idle time to drift back into my old lifestyle. It always started for me, little by little. A little drink here and a little drink there. Then, I would fall back into getting wasted all the time. My church friends would always text me to encourage me during the day, so that helped majorly.

I worked at the salvage yard for around four years. In that period, God was using me to speak to people and love on them as they came to get parts. That definitely shows how much He loves us. He visits us even at the junk yard!

I was at work one day, driving the tractor, when this guy asked me to lift this car so he could get the tires off. So, I drove over there. As I sat there waiting on him, God began to speak to me about him. I was caught off guard, mainly because I didn't want to step out and share what He was telling me to share. After five minutes, I said, "Okay." I opened the door, jumped off the tractor, and went over to where he was. In a cautious manner, I asked him if he had a church home. The Lord asked me to simply tell him how much he loved the man, but I was afraid, so I put the church speech out there. As soon as I said, *church home*, he said, "I do, but I haven't been going. I've been resisting God every day." Then, I began to share about how God poured His love on me and how His kindness brought me to repentance. It was a total divine appointment for this man. He said, "I'm so encouraged. My name is Paul, by the way. I will stop running today and return to his house where I belong."

Be bold, have courage to share what God has done in your life.

Sharing My Faith

I shared my testimony every chance I got. It was tough for the other guys to hear from me about Jesus when I was living like the devil. Where I live, they call those folks *hypocrites*. I was one of the youngest guys working at the salvage yard, and I had some history playing different roles in some Hollywood movies that were being filmed in Shreveport. My experience in the movie industry was playing as an extra in many small films. I got to met Martin Lawrence on the set of 2008 film, *Welcome Home, Roscoe Jenkins*. I also appeared in another 2008 film, *Harold and Kumar*. They were not hearing the story of how God changed my life. All they wanted to hear about was partying, women, and movie stars. I thought about how, in the Bible, it says that a prophet wouldn't be accepted in his hometown (Luke 4:24). That was the truth. I had built a name for myself, and it wasn't "John the Christian." It was "John the party animal."

God often uses the most ordinary people. Sometimes, he uses the toughest criminals. Other times, he uses the most rejected person to carry out his plans. Here's the real deal. If you are willing to see your sin for what it is, you can repent from those ways and walk in His ways. You can become a totally different individual. This is simple but not easy.

Another time when I was working, I saw a guy that I was locked up with. He had been a major influence on me. He looked at me and said, "You still in the Word?" I said, "Everyday." God sent many people there to let me know He was with me and that I was right where I was supposed to be. I continued to serve at church, attend life group, and help other guys that were enrolled in our church's rehab program.

All Things Made New

I met a guy named Jesse at the gym one day when I was hanging out with my boy, Kevin, who was a teacher at our rehab center. Jesse was a young guy that worked with Kevin, and Kevin was determined to get Jesse born again. I had the chance while we were lifting weights to share my testimony with him, and it blew his mind. I began to pick him up

Sundays and Wednesdays for church. Sometimes, I would get him Visine because he would be so high when I picked him up that his eyes would be bloodshot. After a few squirts of cologne and a few drops of Visine, he was set to go. I did this for about a year, and I began to see God restore this man to better than new! Jesse had no idea where his kids and wife were because of their level of addiction.

My experience with ministering to Jesse helped me to see that all I went through was to be able to help other people go through their struggles and show them the way out. I had never felt so much purpose in my life. My past embarrassments, failures, struggles, strongholds, and addictions were being used to greatly help others find purpose and destiny in their lives. Mind blowing, I know.

The Single Life

On the flip side, I was still single. I had never been single very long in my life. This was actually the longest I had ever been single before. I was determined to do this the right way, though. I didn't want to do this halfway. God gave me a fresh start, and I wanted to make good with His opportunity. I grabbed a piece of paper and began to write down the things I wanted in a mate: hair color, skin tone, body type, ethnic background, personality, etc. That's right. I knew that God had the best for me. I kept this in my Bible. If I was going to read and live this, I was going to have goals to do it for. If I ever wondered why I was serving, going to church, attending life group, or making hard decisions when tempted, I referred back to my goals sheet. I want God's best. I want to see my dreams come true. I want to be free from all bondages. I want to be a better leader. Motivation is where it starts and where it will end. The moment you forget why, that's the moment you will quit. As I matured in my relationship with God, I began to make it about Him and not me.

I still was hanging on to some things that I needed to let go of. But, I mean, everyone has their few things that they are supposed to just tolerate... so I thought.

Career Shift

I gave my two-weeks notice at the salvage yard to go work for the Mazda/Porsche dealership in the auto body department. This seemed to be a great fit. Little did I know, the manager was going to quit the first week I started work. As a result, the financial promises he made were not going to happen. My check was a joke.

There was no way I could pay my bills with this job, so I called my friend Jesse over to help me figure this out. We wrote down all my bills and the money I needed to bring home. Then, we put both our hands on that paper and prayed, "Lord, you know all things, and we need a miracle. In spite of a bad decision that was made, bail me out. We love you. Amen." Simple as that, Jack. The very next morning, the Toyota dealership's body shop called and wanted me to start the next day. Of course, I went, and it was a perfect fit job. It was the best job I've had so far!

At this time, I was compromising in the area of relationships. I had been single for three years; that was an absolute miracle. So, I began to help God out by checking out prospects. I met a girl that was beautiful, and she did the church scene, so I was hooked. I began to talk to her. Slowly, she pulled me to her world instead of me pulling her into my world. Next thing I know, I became convinced that church was a dead end road.

Running from God's Love... Again

My mentor called me several times to check on me. I always said I was doing great. I was at one of our rehab support group meetings with Eagle Creek Recovery Center, and I looked at him, and he looked at me. We both knew we wouldn't see each other after this meeting for a long time. I left there and went straight to a buddy's house and began to drink again heavily. This began my next prodigal son season. As Solomon said, "As a dog returns to his own vomit, so a fool repeats his folly" (Prov. 26:11). I was like a dog returning to his vomit.

The Bible says it's better for you to not know the truth than to know it and not obey it. I went downhill from here. Quickly, all of the *addition* that I had gained from the Lord began to disappear. My sinful nature took over completely. I spent the next nine months partying and wasting what God had entrusted to me. It was miserable, trying to live like I didn't know the truth about God and the truth about my life and purpose.

The Bible states that God will finish the work He started, so when I blew it big time, He used that as a testimony. Toward the end of my running from God, He told me it's time to come home. This was a Friday. I had a girlfriend I was living with, so this was going to be a transition. I tried to start a fight so it would look like just a normal breakup. It wasn't that easy. I told her the truth and said God has called me to serve him, and I've been running. She didn't understand, but she respected that.

The next night, I drank and drank and drank until I was basically comatose. My friends found me in the driver seat of my truck, parked in the middle of downtown with my keys in the ignition. The door was still wide open. I'm really not sure how I made it there safely. When they found me, they took me home and called the paramedics to check my pulse and heart rate because of all the Red Bulls and vodka I drank. I was totally unresponsive.

I do remember waking up at 9:00am that Sunday, feeling a little different. I began ironing my clothes for church. I jumped in my truck, very cloudy in my mind but determined that I was going to God's house no matter what.

Part 5

The Joy of Addition

When I walked back into church after being away for so long, I sat to the side. I felt like I was back home after being gone on a long trip. Peace began to flood my soul. I began to think about this scripture verse: "Oh what joy for those whose disobedience is forgiven, whose sin is put out of sight!" (Psa. 32:1) People would glance at me and smile, making my shame dissipate. When it was over, all my friends welcomed me back with open and loving arms. I just wept, having believed a lie during the past nine months, the lie that God didn't have my best in mind and that I could somehow find a better life outside of the house of God.

One of our pastors I was really close with, Pastor Jones, had become a father figure to me while I attend church over the years. My Dad was involved in my life, but we lost touch due to my sinful lifestyle. During the times when I needed him, he wasn't there for me. I was not receptive to any sort of correction from any adult, so that made it hard for him to be Dad to me. Because I felt rejection from him, I felt justified in giving him the same rejection he gave me so he could feel my pain.

Pastor Jones was a great man of God and role

model for me to watch, so when I returned back in the church, my friend Gabriel took me around to his car where his family was standing by. I proceeded to open the door. With a face full of tears, I walked toward them, and they embraced me like I was their own Jones' boy. They wept with me and loved me like a son and friend. Pastor Jones said, "Man, we've been praying for you to come home, and here you are! God is good!"

I smelled like a vodka factory that day, yet I decided that I would do whatever it took to stay connected to God's house and His people. I gathered my belongings from my friend's house where I was sleeping on the couch for that period of time, prepared to move forward with God's plan for my life.

Are you attending church but have not yet gotten involved? Try a life group. Try the choir out.

Do you know someone that needs to be mentored? Begin to help them as you grow.

Are you tired of the same ole job? Try getting a new perspective. Find out what promotions are available.

A Fresh Start

I moved into my parents' house as a 27-year-old man, which was super humbling. I really was okay with it, though. It gave me a chance to restore my relationship with them that was lost from my childhood. We began to meet in the living room on Mondays to talk about the Bible and to share what God was doing in each of our lives. This was very impactful for me, just seeing my parents open up and watch me be transformed by God day after day, month after month, and year after year.

I got to start over with my family on a fresh slate. I honored them because I wanted to, and the Bible says to honor your father and mother and you will be given long life. I actually wanted to do this just so they could benefit—not for any reward. I had been so awful, disrespectful, dishonoring, and unloving to my parents for most of my life. This was God's opportunity to make things right with them and get their blessing plus His blessing.

I returned to my Bible study where I first began with my friends, Miguel and Caitlin. They were with me from the beginning. This couple had a special connection for people that needed to see what Christian married people look like. So much love. So much grace. So much acceptance.

At the Bible study, this Scripture stuck out me

to me the most: "The spirit of the Lord God is upon me, because the Lord has anointed me to preach good tidings to the poor: he has sent me to heal the brokenhearted, to proclaim liberty to captives, and the opening of the prison to those who are bound" (Isa. 61:1). One evening, I was at home, and I had given all the major areas of my life to the Lord as He would ask. However, nicotine was my only area I held on to. I never could get free in this area.

God, being as good as He is, made me a trade. I was reading one night, and I felt in my heart God saying, "If you quit smoking, I'll begin to give you a prophetic dream life." Nicotine was the first drug I picked up and the last one I laid down. Well, I thought it meant dream life in my everyday living. I didn't know that literally meant dreams at night in my sleep. So, I began to have dreams every night— wild dreams. I would write them down. I still would give in to my desire to smoke or dip occasionally, but I would be so disappointed in myself, and I would get mad and continue to try quitting. My friend, Ben, was speaking about addictions and how you can be set free by the power of God, but then you have to walk it out. You have to be responsible and make hard choices to stay free. He made a statement I would never forget. He said, "If God's power wiped all your sins away, all your shame away, and all your guilt away, then what else would it not wipe away? I immediately knew that if I was set free from alcohol and drugs, I definitely didn't have to struggle with nicotine. That day was the last day I would ever use nicotine for the rest of my life.

By this time, I began to attend another life group. Miguel and Caitlin served me very well, teaching me how to be responsible and to make the essential decisions to get the ball rolling again in my life. At Matt's and Britnye's life group, they taught me what it looks like to be a son of God, how to serve the local church, how to receive instruction, how to be teachable, and how to get God's very best in my life.

Future Mate Revealed

One night, I had a dream that a girl named Christine from my church and life group was going to be my wife. So, I wrote it down. The next night, I had the same dream. Again, I wrote it down. On the following night, I had the same dream. Looks like a pattern. Hopefully, I got the point right. The Lord began to remind me of this Bible verse: "So then, they are no longer two but one flesh. Therefore what God has joined together, let no man separate" (Matt. 19:6).

Well, my pattern was not to always do the right thing but to do the wrong thing. So, this was a challenge for me. I shared the dreams with Matt and Britnye. They were so gracious to help me see that dreams can be tricky, so just keep doing what you know to do, and everything will line itself up as long as I do my part. So, I did just that. I didn't focus on what I didn't have. I focused on what I had and made the best of it.

One day, while I was at work painting cars at the Toyota dealership, I felt that it was time to ask Christine out on a date. Well, that was awesome because I kept asking the Lord to reveal the right timing. Like a very excited male, I gathered up the courage to text her to see what she was doing that evening. The only communications I had with Christine during the four years of our friendship were things like "hey," "bye," and "see you later." Two years before I asked her out, I started having the dreams about her being my wife.

I texted her, not even thinking this was asking her out. I really just wanted to know if she was busy or not, so when I asked her in-person, I would know she was available. It's called the non-rejection approach. Well, she texted me back, "Do u need to talk or is this asking me out through a text?" Oh my gosh! I was on the floor!

My friend Ben calls and says, "Hey, let me help you a little bit with this." This was a good thing because my track record with women was horrible. I was never taught how to treat a woman. I pretty much learned all my lessons from the streets. One evening, I got the courage up after being schooled on how to approach a godly woman to ask her on a date. We met at a restaurant named Chiantis. This place was top shelf. I was so nervous that I almost swallowed my tongue. Neither of us had been on a date in years. I wasn't going to go on a date until I knew that I would possibly marry this person and that she felt the same way. Well, I let her know that night that I was interested in her as we enjoyed our dinner and conversation. She made it known that she noticed there was a little interest, so I'm dying over here, wondering if she liked me back. I didn't want to be pushy, so I played it cool. I gave her space and just learned how to be her best friend. This was great ground to grow together. It was easy and comfortable for both of us.

How is your relationship with your Mom and Dad? If your relationship isn't doing well, how can you make things right with them? A letter? A conversation over dinner?

Are you searching for your future mate? Write a description down and pray for her/him?

Beginning a Life Group

I started a men's life group where I invited guys from our church to come and grow together every week. We would pray together, talk about issues, talk about life, cook some great food, play music, be a big brother to each other, watch movies, and worship together at my house. It was so fun meeting every Thursday night and just sharing my struggles and listening to theirs. I watched God build mighty men of faith in the middle of their weakest moments.

There was a very special guy that I got close to from our rehab named Shane Clemons. Words can't say how close we were. Shane was addicted to crack cocaine for 13 years. He was the best artist I had ever seen. He had been down a long road. As an only child, his parents bought him anything and everything he wanted: a top fuel drag car, muscle cars, crotch rockets, paint & body shop, etc. Shane would pawn all this stuff for crack in a New York minute. Shane spent 9 years in the penitentiary where he was in a gang while he spent his time. "Blood in, blood out" is how they operated. He was a member of the Aryan brotherhood for 9 years.

When Shane got out, his addiction took over his life. He found himself at our rehab to begin the restoration process yet again. A great legend named Ben told me once that most men are used to the "build up, tear down" process. As I saw Shane walking down the halls of our church, I saw great destiny in him. I told him, "You are going to start coming to my life group." This guy wasn't a very clean-cut fellow, so this was a bold moment for me. He was about 6'0", 293 lbs., and was covered in tattoos. From the wrist up, both of his arms were covered in jailhouse tats. He had a big demon under his ear and down his back and chest. "White pride" was stamped on his calf muscles on each side. I believed God had a purpose that was greater than his failures! I'm telling you that he would show up every Thursday and take notes when I shared. I would see him at church, worshipping with his hands lifted high and tears streaming down his face, the most beautiful sight any mentor could see.

Shane's best friend was an African American guy named Jeremiah. That was a miracle, considering Shane's previous hatred of other ethnic groups before he accepted Christ. One evening, Shane took Jeremiah to his parents' home. This was the first time an African American person had ever walked into the Clemons home. From that day forward, that family has never been the same because of what God did in Shane and through Shane. He broke racial barriers. He broke chains of addiction. He broke the stereotype of a one-time bound, broken, limited, tatted-up young man and became God's son forever.

Laying a Warrior to Rest

One evening, I was at life group, and I got a phone call from one of the pastors. I knew something must be wrong, so I stepped outside. In my mind, I knew this wasn't about to be good. The voice on the other line was hesitant to speak.

He said, "John?"

"Yes, Sir. It's me."

"I have some bad news for you, buddy," my pastor said.

I replied, "Okay, I believe I'm ready."

He continued, "Your friend, Shane, was found dead in his room today, and his parents are about to call you. They need you, man."

I was really trying to be strong in the moment, but I just sat down in my friend's driveway and cried silently as the phone calls came in one by one.

I had the privilege to help with Shane's funeral

in Texas where he was buried. When we got back in town from the funeral, I began to put together a service for Shane, involving all his friends he made here in Louisiana. We put all his pictures up in the walkway and had a very close friend sing the songs Shane loved to hear from her. Then, there were different people that knew Shane that wanted to come up and speak. I came up at the end to honor my boy, Shane, whom I had so much time and life invested in. He loved to come to my house and talk.

One night, Shane told me that all he ever prayed for was to see his parents know Jesus like he did. I never forgot that. Time went on, and his parents and I kept close contact. Shane's parents, Marc and Judy, called me one day and told me they had given their lives to Jesus at church. I couldn't believe how good God was in that moment. I was so full of joy! Great victory does come out of tragedy still!

Shane went home to be with the Lord on September 23, 2011. He had double pneumonia and was found in his bedroom on his knees, face down on the bed, reading his Bible with worship music playing. There is no doubt that Shane knew it was his time. There is not a Thursday that goes by that I don't look across my living room and think about seeing his face. I've met many broken men and watched them pile in my living room, then seasons later, see them living the good life that Christ died for them to have.

What to me seemed so tragic was an answered prayer for Shane even though he was in heaven. In August 2013, I had the great privilege of baptizing his parents. Shane would have been so proud of them. He also would have had some jokes to add for them as well.

Growing Together

Christine and I served as the directors of the Crew ministry at church before and during our courtship. As a reminder, the Crew does a little of everything during a church service. We get the microphones ready, get waters for singers, run the projectors, run the lights, carry instruments, set changes, etc. We run anywhere from 15-26 people on this crew. This ministry is a great opportunity for people to serve their church. The team members range from 18 to 50 years old. We act as a family within a family.

Christine and I would take time outside of our schedule on Saturdays and go fishing. This didn't work out well for me all the time because she knew how to catch fish without even trying. On one occasion, we went to this lake where a friend of mine was catching some big fish. I got lost on the way there, so after two hours of driving, I pulled up to a little stop-and-go store to grab some minnows so we could do a little bank fishing. Well, Christine throws her minnow in the water and bam! She catches a catfish! Let me tell you something. She didn't want to touch the fish, so I had to take her fish off the line and then re-bait her hook so I could get back to my rod to try to catch one for myself. Before I caught my first fish, she caught her second! I showed excitement for her but little did she know, I almost cut her line with my pocket knife. Yes, we loaded up right after I got out-fished by her. I figured that, by now, she might as well be my girlfriend after she out-fished me. So, after a nice walk by the riverbank downtown Shreveport, we made it official and informed our close friends while we enjoyed some coffee at Starbucks. We were now "boyfriend and girlfriend."

Are you in a relationship? Go do an activity together outside. It could bring refreshment to you both.

Are you involved at church? If not, start today. Find a place to serve. You will never regret it.

No More Pain

"The Investigator" was my Aunt Sarah's nickname. She was a mother to me ever since I was child. I would stay at her house all the time. She lived in a very rough neighborhood. She always stayed on me and my friends about not doing drugs, but we never listened. She would find all kinds of stuff around her house. We always felt that she was one of the boys even though she preached so hard to us to just have a good time without drugs. Her house is where I would throw massive parties. During my whole life, I always took care of her. I grocery shopped for her, mowed her grass, fixed all the house problems, and worked on her cars. I was pretty much her child from birth.

Aunt Sarah began to have health problems, mainly because she didn't take good care of herself. She had a heart attack, and the doctors diagnosed her with congestive heart failure. The doctors recommended that she get the surgery to have it fixed, but my Aunt Sarah was as tough as nails. She would fight anybody, especially a doctor. She told me straight up, "John, I won't have that surgery done. Bottom line. I am 59 years old, and I won't let them cut me open anymore." When she said something, Jack, you could take it to the bank. I would have to take her to the hospital late at night because of the swelling in her ankles. Then, it would pass for a while, and I would have to do it again.

One evening, I was driving down Youree Drive. A staff member from the hospital my aunt had been in and out of for months for heart problems called and said, "You need to get here ASAP. Your aunt's condition has gotten worse." We flew up to Willis Knighton Hospital, but by the time we arrived, it was too late. She had passed away. She died from congestive heart failure.

I was a mess. Man, she was my rock for years, like a second mom to me. I held it together for the family. We got all the arrangements set up for her. Then, the day to bury her came along. I was honored to be able to do her benediction at the grave site. This was a rough time for me. I had trouble getting past losing her, but I was glad I had the opportunity to share the gospel with her after living such a ruthless life for so many years.

Have you lost a close friend or family member? Reminiscing about them with others brings joy.

Is there anyone that has been there for you time and time again that you need to be thankful for?

Playing Jesus

About that time, Easter was rolling around. We have a major Easter production at the church. I was given the privilege of playing the role of Jesus in the production. Christine was the director up top, and the crew was in place to help with all the stage sets. The play had a great turn out, and 84 people gave their lives to Jesus. At the very end, I stepped out of the tomb where our pastor asked me where I met Jesus. My response was that I met Jesus in a jail cell where He set me free. It was a very solid production, and all the actors did amazing.

Addition in the Midst of Adversity

The next week rolled around, and our friends, the Jones, were launching their new music album at a release concert at the church. I was up there early Sunday morning, getting it all ready to go with the Crew team. I was trying to see the amps under the stage, but I couldn't get to my flash light. I tried to squeeze myself through this small opening when I felt something pop. It felt like a muscle popped. I didn't pay too much attention to it.

Church was starting, so I hurried down to my seat. I began to feel weird, like something was maybe wrong with my body. We have communion at church every Sunday, so I took my juice and cracker came back to my seat. I prayed while taking my communion, and then I began to sweat. I was thinking, "Oh no! What was in that juice? Was that cracker bad?"

I slipped out of my seat and headed to the car. While I was walking, I texted Christine, "Something is wrong with my body." I walked out to my truck, sweating profusely. I cranked it up and put the air conditioning on full blast and then I saw Christine walking toward me. Then, bam! Lights out! I had my eyes wide open, but it was pitch black. I started banging on the side of the truck with my arm yelling, "Help! Help! Help!" I could hear Christine yelling, "I need a paramedic to the parking lot." I said, "Baby, pray for me. I think I'm about to die."

Within minutes, a crowd came outside with a crash cart and began running an IV into my arm. My vision returned. Then, I started feeling this pain in my left side by my lung. When the ambulance arrived, they began to put stuff on my chest. Then, they saw that my skin was yellow, which meant that I was bleeding internally, so they floored it.

So, for the past hour and half, I was bleeding internally because my spleen was ruptured. I lost 800cc of blood, which dropped my blood count down to 9. They rushed me into emergency surgery.

The surgeon removed my spleen and sewed me straight up the middle, putting 39 staples in my stomach. Jesus was whipped with 39 lashes, so immediately I knew God was with me in this when I counted the 39. Having no spleen meant no immune system for the rest of my life. No matter how much better I got, I would still be susceptible to getting sick easily.

That day, if Christine hadn't come outside at the second she did, I would have died in my truck all alone. My recovery from the surgery took me three months to get back to operating normally. Finally, I went back to painting cars, which is what I loved to do. I adjusted well back to work and the environment. I took my daily vitamins and got shots when I needed them. This kept my immunity high. I drank healthy drinks and ate healthy food the best I could.

Have you ever encountered death?

How good has God been to you? Write a story about it.

Wedding Bells

On September 23, 2012, Christine and I were fishing in this cove on Cypress Lake early one morning when I asked her to marry me. As we sat in my Jon boat, I sang a song for her, which was the first song I had ever written. The Lord gave it to me for her. She just cried. I didn't know if it was because she was happy or if my singing hurt her ears. She said, "Yes," to my proposal, so I caught the biggest fish of my lifetime that day.

From that day on, we enjoyed time together as an engaged couple. We planned a gorgeous wedding, filled with all our close friends and family. It is so easy to lose the meaning of this special season of engagement as it can be swept away by emotion. We were blessed to have plenty of leaders in our lives to help us make the best of our time.

We got married in same place we met and continued to grow as friends. We went to Hawaii on our honeymoon, and it was the most beautiful place I've ever been. When we returned, we both stayed at the job for a period of time. Then, Christine transitioned into a role working for our church as a bookkeeper.

Meanwhile, I began to have more health issues. This time, it was a food allergy, so I missed many days at work. I would get major migraines from any food that had any oil besides olive oil in it, which is a ton of foods. This allowed me to transition to trusting God to come through for us financially. We had no plans, nor did I have any jobs lined up. It was a total step of faith.

A few weeks later, I received a notice that a very close family to us offered to build me a brand new auto body shop to begin working out of! We named the business, "Quality Paint & Body." We immediately began the process of launching it for our city. Immediately, I received a letter in the mail, stating that all my past debts had been paid in full! So, God chose to cancel all my debts in just seven years of serving him wholeheartedly, reminding me of this verse: "And Moses commanded them saying: at the end of every seven years, in the set time of the year of release, at the feast of tabernacles" (Deut. 31:10).

Shortly after that, we got a major financial blessing through the mail to help us in the tough times. If that wasn't enough, I got an opportunity to go with Pastor Denny to Bayou Dorcheat Correction Center to share my testimony to 450 prisoners.

God did it for me, and He will do it for you! God is good all the time, and all the time, God is good! He's good even when we can't physically see it with our eyes. Always believe that the best is on its way in your life, no matter what the outcome. Let me share something with you that you should never forget as long as you live: You may have started off in life wrong, but through Christ, your life can be restored to finish very, very well.

How do you plan to propose to your mate when the time is right?

What trials have you been through? God will use all the sufferings to help build his kingdom through you.

Have you ever just trusted God when you had nothing to lean on but him?

Do you have dreams? What will you do to see them come to pass? Go for it!

Testimonies of Addiction to Addition

Ben

Ben was 12 years old when he first started using drugs. By the time he was 21, he was addicted to crack cocaine, pills, and methamphetamines. He became an intravenous drug user. Ben was set free by the power of Jesus Christ and has been fully restored to a brand new life. He has been totally free for 12 years and has gained major ground in life with his wife Melandy and their two beautiful boys. He was the dean of students at Evangel Christian Academy. He also went to college to get his bachelor's degree in Psychology so that he could become a Christian counselor. He has also completed Bible college to help him equip young men and women to be disciples of Jesus. Ben is currently the Director at Eagle Creek Recovery Center.

Alex

Alex started his life out by riding BMX bikes with kids older than him. Around the age of 13, he started smoking marijuana out of peer pressure, which led him to another drug, alcohol. For years, Alex medicated himself with alcohol and pills. He was drinking around one liter of liquor per day, finding himself constantly in and out of trouble with the law. He came to Eagle Creek for recovery where he was able to get some temporary help but soon returned back to his old life choices. He once again came through the doors of the recovery center more serious this time, having escaped major jail time for his alcohol and drug addiction behavior. Alex said,

"This time, being plugged into the Word made a huge difference. I told the Lord I was spiritually bankrupt, so I read the Bible cover-to-cover one evening. It captivated me so much I couldn't wait to get back in the evenings to read more. The Word has been changing my heart and actions lately. I clean up my own messes now. I actually do my chores. I feel conviction when I do the smallest things wrong, so I correct them quickly. I never did that before."

Alex went on to say, "Staying plugged in to accountability, your Bible, and church has been the key this time around." At the time of this writing, Alex has been free from his addictions for seven days. He is still in the recovery program and is hoping to be in the Transitional Living Center at the end of his 90-day term.

Darren

Darren was 34 when he began to experience addiction as a high school football coach. He had to have emergency surgery for diverticulitis where they had to remove some of his intestines. For recovery, they gave him some pain medication that would forever change his life. He became dependent on the pills, which led him to start taking money from the football equipment account to support his pill addiction. This didn't last long before he was caught trying to cover up all he was stealing.

The school administration chose to show him grace. They sat him down and asked him to go into a rehab program. They chose Eagle Creek for him to come and receive his treatment. Darren says he had been to other programs before but never embraced the "God part." When he came, he had just enough brokenness and willingness to accept the truths he needed to hear. He said,

> "[During the program] I found out that I was believing a lie for so many years. I believed that my identity was in labels, my job, what I thought I needed. The only thing I needed was Christ as my identity. This truth began to bring great healing and restoration to my life."

Darren is now in the Transitional Living Center after completing his 90 days in the treatment program.

CPSIA information can be obtained
at www.ICGtesting.com
Printed in the USA
FFOW02n1421010414
4556FF